HOW It's MADE

A Cotton T-Shirt

Sarah Ridley

GARETH**STEVENS**
PUBLISHING
A Member of the WRC Media Family of Companies

The author and publishers would like to thank Gossypium for their help with this book.

Please visit our web site at: **www.garethstevens.com**
For a free color catalog describing Gareth Stevens Publishing's list of high-quality books
and multimedia programs, call 1-800-542-2595 (USA) or 1-800-387-3178 (Canada).
Gareth Stevens Publishing's fax: (414) 332-3567.

Library of Congress Cataloging-in-Publication Data

Ridley, Sarah, 1963- .
    A cotton T-shirt / Sarah Ridley.
      p. cm. — (How it's made)
    Includes index.
    ISBN 0-8368-6294-5 (lib. bdg.)
    1. T-shirts—Juvenile literature.   2. Cotton—Juvenile literature   I. Title.
TT675.R54   2006
687'.115—dc22   2005054074

This North American edition first published in 2006 by
Gareth Stevens Publishing
A Member of the WRC Media Family of Companies
330 West Olive Street, Suite 100
Milwaukee, WI 53212 USA

This U.S. edition copyright © 2006 by Gareth Stevens, Inc.
Original edition copyright © 2005 by Franklin Watts.
First published in Great Britain in 2005 by Franklin Watts,
96 Leonard Street, London EC2A 4XD, United Kingdom.

Series editor: Sarah Peutrill
Art director: Jonathan Hair
Designer: Jemima Lumley

Gareth Stevens editor: Barbara Kiely Miller
Gareth Stevens art direction: Tammy West
Gareth Stevens graphic designer: Charlie Dahl

Photo credits: (t=top, b=bottom, l=left, r=right, c=center)
Bill Barksdale/AG Stock USA/Alamy: 9t. Nigel Cattlin/Holt Studios: 7tr, 26cl. Bob Daemmrich/Image Works/Topham: 6b.
Geri Engberg/Image Works/Topham: 16tr. David Frazier/Image Works/Topham: 11t. Gossypium: front cover (both), back cover
(both), 1, 4 (both), 5t, 6t, 7tl, 8, 9b, 10 (both), 12 (both), 13t, 14, 15t, 16bl, 19b, 20 (both), 21tl, 21bl, 22, 23t, 24 (both), 26tl, 26bl,
26tr, 26cr, 26br, 27cl, 27bl, 27tr, 27cr, 27br. Oldrich Karasek/Still Pictures: 18t, 27tl. Bob Krist/Corbis: 18b. Mary Evans Picture
Library: 13b, 15b, 25. Novosti/Topham: 7b. Picturepoint/Topham: 11b, 21br. UPP/Topham: 29t. Watts: 17b, 19t, 23b, 28 (all), 31
(all). Peter Wilson/Holt Studios: 30r. Michael S. Yamashita/Corbis: 30l.

Printed in the United States of America

1 2 3 4 5 6 7 8 9 10 09 08 07 06

Words that appear in the glossary are printed in
boldface type the first time they occur in the text.

Contents

Most T-shirts are made of cotton.

Making a cotton T-shirt starts when cotton fibers are picked from plants on a farm. Cotton plants grow fibers that are made into cotton **textiles**. After the cotton is harvested, or picked, many people are needed to turn the cotton fibers into a T-shirt.

This T-shirt is made from a knitted cotton textile. Other names for a textile are cloth, fabric, and material.

Thousands of cotton fibers grow inside each cotton boll, or seed pod.

Cotton plants need plenty of warm weather and rain to grow well, so farmers plant **cotton seeds** before a rainy season begins. One or two weeks after planting, cotton seedlings begin to poke their leaves above the soil.

On a small cotton farm, cows might be used to pull equipment.

World Cotton Producers

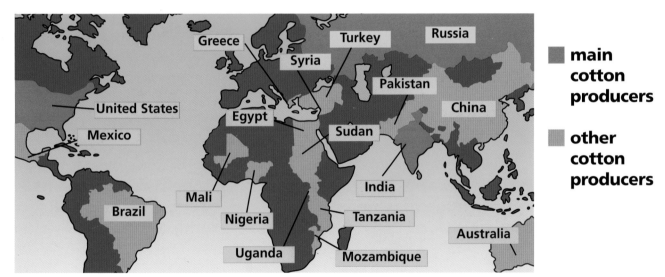

Greece
Turkey
Russia
Syria
Pakistan
United States
Egypt
China
Mexico
Sudan
India
Mali
Brazil
Nigeria
Tanzania
Uganda
Mozambique
Australia

■ main cotton producers

■ other cotton producers

Why cotton?

Cotton is a good material to use for making clothes. Cotton threads can be woven or knit together to make very strong cloth, or fabric. Cotton will not tear easily or wear out quickly. Because it is strong, cotton can be made into either fine, light cloth or thick, heavy cloth, such as denim, which is used to make jeans.

Cotton farmers water their plants.

Cotton plants in places with long rainy seasons usually get plenty of water. In dry areas, farmers use **irrigation** to make sure their cotton plants have enough water. They have special equipment to water the plants, or they lay pipes along the sides of the fields to carry water to the plants' roots.

To help cotton plants grow, a farmer will remove weeds.

This large farm uses huge machines to irrigate cotton fields.

After growing for three or four months, the cotton plants burst into flower. The flowers are white or pink, depending on the type of cotton plant.

A cotton plant in flower

After a few days, the flower petals fall off, and green pods, called cotton bolls, start to develop.

At first, cotton bolls are green.

Thirsty Cotton

Cotton plants are very thirsty, and huge cotton farms can use up valuable local water supplies trying to keep their plants healthy. Sometimes, these cotton farms use so much water that rivers and lakes dry up completely.

People started growing cotton around the Aral Sea in Russia about seventy-five years ago. The cotton farms drained all the rivers that once flowed into the sea. Now the sea and the land around it is a dry desert, dotted with abandoned boats.

The farmers check the plants for pests.

While the cotton bolls are growing, farmers watch for pests. If they find any insect damage, they may spray a chemical **pesticide** on the plants to kill the pests.

Organic cotton is grown without chemicals. Organic cotton farmers make natural pesticides from plant substances and cow urine.

This trap attracts harmful insects to keep them away from the cotton plants.

Why grow organic cotton?

Some farmers try to grow as many plants as possible. This kind of **intensive farming** drains the soil of **nutrients** so that farmers must use chemical **fertilizers**. Unless fertilizers are used very carefully, their chemicals can end up in water supplies and in food crops.

Organic farmers grow a variety of crops and use **manure** to fertilize them. They farm without harming the soil. Also, organic farms are usually small, which means that farmers can probably spot pests and diseases before too much damage is done.

As much as 2 gallons (8 liters) of pesticide may be sprayed on a 1 acre (1/2 hectare) field of cotton during the growing season.

What happens on big farms?

When cotton is grown on large, modern farms, the farmers use chemicals to prevent plant diseases and to kill insect pests. If their crops are damaged, the farmers could lose a lot of money. Although chemicals are expensive, they help the farmers harvest much more cotton than organic farms can produce.

Cotton bolls split open about fifty to seventy days after the cotton plant flowers.

Organic farmers may also get rid of pests by using traps or insects that will live on the plants and eat the pests.

When healthy cotton bolls are ripe, they burst open. The fluffy fibers inside the bolls dry in the warm air.

Ripe cotton is harvested.

Workers walk up and down the rows of plants, picking ripe bolls.

Harvesting, or picking, ripe cotton bolls by hand is hard work and takes a long time. Farm workers pile up the picked bolls along the edges of the fields.

Next, the workers remove the fibers from the bolls. At this point, cotton seeds are stuck to the fibers. To separate the seeds from the fibers, the cotton must be sent to a ginning mill.

Workers carry the cotton bolls out of the fields.

What happens on big farms?

When cotton is grown on large farms, farmers use huge machines to harvest their crops. At harvest time, the farmers spray the cotton with a chemical that makes the leaves drop off. Then, harvesting machines pull the bolls off the plants. Inside the machines, the outsides of the bolls are removed, leaving just the cotton fibers with the seeds still attached.

This machine travels row by row, harvesting the cotton in a huge field.

In the Past

Cotton was in great demand in the early 1800s. Many U.S. landowners grew cotton on huge farms called plantations. At that time, all cotton was farmed and picked by hand, which was possible only because the landowners owned slaves — men and women who were brought over from Africa against their will and were forced to work in the cotton fields.

Many thousands of African slaves were brought to the United States to harvest cotton.

The farmers sell their cotton to a ginning mill.

At a ginning mill, a machine removes twigs and dirt from the cotton fibers. Then the cotton seeds need to be separated from the fibers.

Workers unload a shipment of cotton at a ginning mill.

Inside a ginning mill

A machine called a cotton gin is used for this job. When the cotton is fed into the gin, the fibers either stick to the rough surface of a roller or are caught on saws. The machine moves the fibers through a space too small for the seeds to fit, which pulls the seeds away from the fibers.

After the seeds, have been removed, cotton fibers are light and fluffy. Machines press the fibers into big bales, which are sold to spinning mills.

These bales of cotton are ready for a spinning mill.

In the Past

Until 1793, cotton seeds had to be removed from cotton fibers by hand, which took a very long time. Then, in the United States, Eli Whitney invented a machine called the cotton gin to remove the seeds. One person turning the handle of this machine could do as much work as twelve people removing seeds by hand. Later, a larger version of Whitney's machine was connected to a power supply, allowing cotton to be ginned at an amazing speed.

One person can run a Whitney cotton gin alone. This machine separates cotton seeds from cotton fibers.

The cotton arrives at a spinning mill.

Workers at a spinning mill weigh the cotton and check the quality of each bale. A mill often mixes the cotton from different bales to make a better quality cloth.

The mill has machines that do different jobs. One machine sucks cotton fibers up a tube into another machine, called a carding machine. The carding machine lines up fibers to form soft ropes.

Farmers are paid for their cotton by the pound. The bales of cotton are weighed when they arrive at the mill.

Next, a ring spinning machine splits up the long ropes of cotton. It takes several threads of cotton and twists them together tightly to form **yarn**, which is collected on **bobbins**.

Ring spinning machines can turn cotton fibers into yarn in minutes.

In the Past

Before spinning machines were invented, cotton fibers were made into thread on spinning wheels. A spinner tied a thread from a rope of cotton fibers to a pointed rod called a **spindle**. While turning the wheel with one hand, the spinner slowly pulled the rope of cotton away from the wheel with her other hand. The fibers formed a long thread that the spinning wheel twisted together to produce yarn. Some people still spin yarn by hand today.

In this drawing from 1823, the woman on the right is spinning cotton fibers into thick thread, which the woman on the left then spins into fine thread.

Cotton yarn is sent to a textile factory.

At a textile factory, cotton yarn is made into cloth. Workers put bobbins of yarn on knitting machines that loop together, or knit, the yarn into cotton cloth. The way these machines knit is similar to the way people knit by hand, but the machines are much faster. This kind of knitting equipment has as many as 2,500 needles on one machine.

A young knitter uses knitting needles to pull one loop of yarn through another.

The mechanical arms above knitting machines also pull loops of yarn through each other to knit cotton threads into cloth.

Knitting or weaving?

T-shirts are made of knitted cotton, a material made by linking cotton loops together. Many other kinds of clothes are made of woven cotton. Using a frame called a loom, cotton yarn is crisscrossed over and under lengths of other yarn to form a block of cloth.

In this example of weaving (*right*), the blue thread passes under the first red thread, over the next one, then under the next, and so on. In every other row, the blue thread will do just the opposite.

Why cotton?

Cotton is a good fabric for clothing because it keeps us cool. Each cotton fiber is hollow inside so air can move easily from one side of the fiber to the other. The movement of air in cotton clothing helps the wearer feel cool. Cotton also soaks up moisture. For this reason, it is often used to make bath towels and bedsheets.

The cotton cloth is dyed to make it a different color.

Before dyeing cotton cloth, factory workers wash it in hot, soapy water. Then they choose a dye color. Dyes contain chemical powders or liquids that add color to textiles.

Powdered dyes come in every color a T-shirt maker might want to use.

In the Past

Textiles used to be colored with natural dyes made from insects or plants. The crushed shells of cochineal insects, for example, make a pink dye. Dye made from the roots of madder plants turns cloth red. Different plants are used to make other colors. Natural dyes are not used very often today because the colors fade quickly when clothes are washed. Some textile producers in rural areas, however, still use natural dyes.

Cochineal insects are specially farmed so they can be used to make pink dye.

Why cotton?

Because many people like to wear colorful clothes, it is helpful that cotton is easy to dye. Without dye, all our cotton clothes would be various shades of white. Cotton cloth can be dyed in different ways. This T-shirt (*right*) has been tie-dyed. Small areas of the shirt were tied up tightly with rubber bands or string so that dye could not get into them. After the shirt was dyed and dried, the bands were taken off, leaving areas of cloth without color.

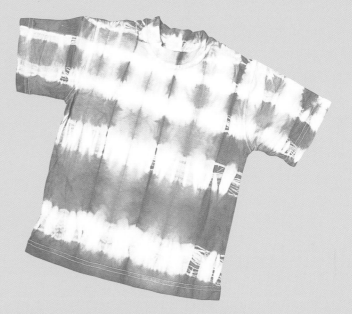

Workers fill a large container with water, mix in the dye, and put the cloth into the container. A chemical is added to the dye so the color will not wash out when clothes made from the cloth are cleaned. Finally, the cloth is put into huge drying machines.

This cloth is dyed pink in the colored water, then it is pulled out onto rollers.

Workers cut out and sew the T-shirt.

The cloth goes to a garment factory where workers spread it over tables and cut it into the pieces needed to make the T-shirt. Some pieces are cut by hand, others by a machine.

A machine controlled by a computer cuts out pieces of cloth in the correct sizes and shapes to make T-shirts.

The various pieces of the T-shirt are put together by a worker who has his or her own sewing machine.

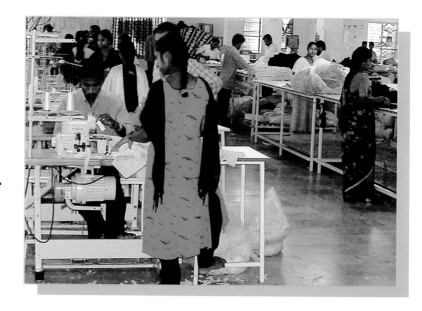

Hundreds of people work in this factory, making T-shirts and other clothes.

The worker uses the sewing machine to attach the front piece of the T-shirt to the back piece, to add the sleeves, and to trim the neck opening.

Each T-shirt is checked after all pieces have been sewn together.

Six feet (2 meters) of soil were needed to grow the cotton used to make this T-shirt.

In the Past

During the 1700s and 1800s, many children worked in mills that made cotton textiles. Mill owners paid the children much less per week than they paid adults. Small children had to crawl under machines that were running to repair them or to clean up. Sometimes, accidents happened, and children died. Many of the children became sick because the air they had to breathe was full of cotton fluff and chemicals.

In the 1800s, many children in the United States spent most of the day working in textile mills. Laws limiting child labor were not passed until the early 1900s.

A design is printed on the T-shirt.

This blue T-shirt is stretched tightly on a printing machine, ready for a screen to be lowered onto it and colored ink to be applied.

One way to put designs on T-shirts is a method called screen printing. The T-shirt is held firmly in place on the flat surface of a printing machine. Above the T-shirt is a screen — a frame with material stretched across it that has a design marked out in small holes. The screen is lowered onto the T-shirt and colored ink is pressed through the holes in the screen. If a design has more than one color, another screen is used, and the process is repeated for each color.

After the ink on a T-shirt design is dry, a machine sews printed labels inside the T-shirt. The labels tell how the T-shirt should be washed, where it was made, and for which manufacturer.

Which of these T-shirts would you want to wear?

Why cotton?

The same kind of cotton cloth can be made to look very different simply by using different printing methods or by adding **embroidery**. Repeated patterns can be printed by using wood blocks into which designs have been carved. Putting a design on a roller allows the same picture to be printed over and over again. Using colored threads, pictures can be embroidered, or sewn, onto cloth.

This colorful cotton bag is decorated with embroidery.

A printed pattern has been repeated to cover all sides of this cotton bag.

The T-shirt arrives at stores ready to be sold.

When shipments of T-shirts arrive in stores, workers iron the shirts and hang them up with other clothes that are for sale.

Some people may buy a T-shirt after looking at a photo of it in a catalog or on a computer, but most people go to a store to buy a T-shirt. At a store, a person can try on the T-shirt to make sure it fits and take the T-shirt home that same day.

Will this customer buy the T-shirt featured in this book?

Store owners shop for T-shirts, too. They have to look at designs and decide which T-shirts they want to sell and how many to order. Some store owners will sell only T-shirts made from cotton grown by farmers who have been paid a fair price for their crops.

In the Past

Before cotton was widely available, people wore clothes made from wool, linen, or silk, depending on how much money they had. Because clothes were expensive, some people could afford only a few pieces. Their clothes often smelled because washing and drying wool clothing was difficult. By the 1600s, cotton was inexpensive enough in the United States for most people to own more than one set of clothes. Cotton changed people's lives.

Three women washing clothes in the 19th century

How a T-shirt Is Made.

1. Farmers plant cotton seeds and water the growing plants.

4. The ripe cotton is harvested.

2. The cotton plants blossom, then the flowers drop off.

5. Workers carry the cotton to collection points.

3. Cotton pods, or bolls, grow where the flowers were and split open.

6. The cotton is taken to a ginning mill, where the cotton seeds are removed.

9. The white cotton cloth is dyed a new color.

10. Workers cut out the pieces of the T-shirt and sew them together.

8. At a textile factory, a knitting machine knits the yarn into cotton cloth.

11. A design is printed on the T-shirt.

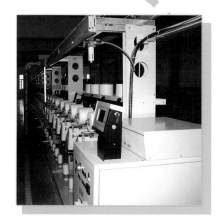

7. The cotton goes to a spinning mill, and a ring spinning machine turns the cotton fibers into yarn.

12. The T-shirt arrives at a store to be sold to a customer.

More Uses for Cotton

A lot of cotton is used to make clothes, but cotton has many other uses, too.

Cotton can be mixed with other kinds of fibers to make stretchy fabrics for swimsuits and socks.

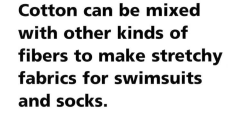

Cotton can be made into towels. Look carefully at a towel to see the loops of cotton.

Cotton is found all around the house — in curtains, cushion covers, and bedsheets. It washes well and lasts a long time.

Bandages that are made of cotton can be washed in very hot water to kill germs.

Cotton can be made into tough canvas for shoes.

How many different things that are made of cotton can you find around your house?

Recycling Cotton

Cotton cloth is made from plants so it will eventually rot away. But instead of putting unwanted clothes in the garbage, they can be given to a charity or to someone you know who will wear them. Even if the clothes have holes in them, they can be recycled. Special factories cut up old clothes or pull out the cotton yarns from the clothes and use them to make new items out of cotton.

A cotton plant produces two crops, not just one. The second crop is the cotton seeds, which can be used to make the following products:

- **cooking oil**
- **animal feed**
- **camera film**
- **soap**
- **garden fertilizer**
- **seeds to plant new cotton crops**

Other Textiles

Plant Fibers

Other kinds of plants besides cotton can be used to make textiles, too. The main ones are linen and hemp.

Linen is made from the stem of the flax plant. Clothes made from linen are comfortable to wear, but they wrinkle more easily than cotton.

Hemp is a plant that can be made into cloth. Hemp plants grow well in many different countries, and they are not attacked by diseases and pests as much as cotton is.

Animal Fibers

Some textiles, such as wool and silk, are made from animal fibers.

Silk comes from a caterpillar's cocoon. A cocoon is the case a caterpillar spins around itself before it changes into a moth. Silk threads make a beautiful, shiny fabric that is soft, strong, and lightweight. Clothes made from silk keep people cool.

Wool is collected from the coats of sheep, goats, rabbits, and even camels. After the wool has been cleaned, it can be spun into thread and knitted or woven to make clothing. Wool sweaters keep people warm.

Manufactured Fibers

Many textiles today are made from manufactured fibers. These fibers are created mainly from coal, oil, or wood.

Polyester (*right*), acrylic, and nylon are manufactured fibers. Because polyester is not expensive, it is often used instead of cotton or is mixed with cotton. Acrylic is often used in place of wool. Because nylon stretches, it is used for tights and other stretchy clothing.

Glossary

bobbins – reels for holding thread

cotton boll – the whole seed pod of the cotton plant, including the cotton fibers

cotton fibers – the thin, hairlike threads that grow inside the boll of a cotton plant

cotton seeds – the small black seeds attached to cotton fibers on a cotton plant

embroidery – designs or decorations made by sewing with a needle and thread

fertilizers – products that are added to soil to increase the nutrients in the soil

intensive farming – the practice of growing as many crops as possible or raising as many animals as possible to sell

irrigation – a system of watering crops using ditches, pipes, or other equipment

manure – solid animal waste that is often used as fertilizer

nutrients – vitamins, minerals, and other substances that help living things grow

organic – grown in a natural environment, without using chemical fertilizers or pesticides

pesticide – a substance that kills insects or other pests

spindle – the long, pointed rod or pin on a spinning wheel that winds and holds thread

textiles – materials made up of threads and fibers. Textiles are also called cloth or fabric.

yarn – the twisted fibers of cotton, wool, or other materials that are knit or woven into cloth

Index